# Sanctified Ambition

*6 Uncommon Lessons on Seeing and
Sensing God Through Success or Failure*

ARVELL CRAIG

# DEDICATION

To my wife Kiem.
For your love, trust, belief,
commitment and support.
Thank you.

# CONTENTS

# PROLOGUE

In the summer of 2007, my life peaked to what felt like a mountain top, but would later descend sharply to over five years of the badlands. Full of ambition and talent, I had no idea that I was still wet behind the ears. Badlands or wilderness, however you want to describe my situation, I had believed I was primed and headed to the Promised Land, but things didn't go as planned. You see, I thought because I had so many things going well, life would only get better. In almost every area I was keeping score, things looked as if I was winning and in control.

Marriage? Check. I was a newlywed with a Christian fairytale story. Guy meets girl while attending church. The two never date, but court, while serving the pastor's family. They pray and quickly realize that it's God's will that they marry. They meet, court, and marry all within the year of their first encounter.

Children? Check. We had our first child within two years of marriage and she was born healthy and strong, without complications. After a few weeks she was sleeping well and showing signs of creativity, independence, and the seeds of an Olympic level hand-eye coordination.

Car? House? Job? Check, Check, Check! It seemed we were on a hot streak with uncommon favor. All in the *holy* year of 2007, we bought a new car and a new house and my job was the best job I'd ever had, paying more than four times my previous work. We gave, tithed, served, and it seemed we were getting our just desserts.

Finally, there was ministry. Big CHECK! I graduated seminary that year and was made associate pastor at a young, vibrant church. I was given the opportunity to conduct my own weekly meetings and exercise all my gifts.

Each of these things, these external areas, these publicly praised and acknowledged spheres of life, made me feel accepted, successful, and valued. But by the summer of the following year, almost everything changed. Without drama or fanfare, our positions in the church ended. My job situation lost its stability when the owner moved away and closed the local office. My identity, tied to church leadership and job security, began to deteriorate, causing a ripple effect of increased stress, fear, and anxiety. Not that I really knew or acknowledged everything. But just as good fruit is produced from a healthy tree, my unhealthy ways of coping were the evidence that not all was well on the inside.

Needless to say, these changes affected the dynamics of my home. So much was changing and yet we weren't secure enough individually or collectively to know how to deal with it all. We had no family to turn to, no friends, advisors, or trusted relationships. Well…maybe we had a few people, thousands of miles away in our respective home towns, but in the day-to-day, week-to-week experiences, we only had each other and surface level interactions at work or church.

Yes, we also had God. But God wasn't speaking. Or we weren't hearing Him. And the disruptions and disappointments continued.

As our daughter grew, we figured it was time to have another child. But pregnancy wasn't as easy the second time. Months turned into years and even with the aid of spiritual and medical intervention, we still couldn't get pregnant. Friends, with whom we celebrated the births of first children, went on to have seconds and thirds, while we just had our hope. Even our daughter, as she grew, learned to ask us and then pray nightly for a little brother or sister. This started out as adorable, but after a year with no baby in mommy's belly, our daughter eventually gave up.

At this point, I still wasn't reflecting on the changes or disappointments. I simply got up each day and tended to the grind. My primary focus was on making money and growing the business I started when the previous job moved away. I had to rely on God and myself to hunt for new clients and fulfill existing obligations. God was dependable, though not always understandable. But as for myself, my discipline and abilities were questionable.

I will admit that there was excitement with living free from bosses and offices, but there was also mounting pressure to not mess it all up. I lived without guarantees, savings, or health insurance. It was just me as chief cook and bottle washer and I managed it the best I could.

As time went on, and months became years, I would sometimes get honest with myself, allow myself to reflect about how I really felt. The feelings spanned disappointment, offense, and hurt. I felt confused, conflicted, and condemned with how I lived each day, divorced from what I thought I was meant to do. There wasn't any clear path to live out my dreams, talents, and perceived purpose. I ran a business because I had to, not because I wanted to. To keep my heart engaged, I would stuff my feelings and rationalize my actions.

I resolved that growing a business instead of a church was God's sovereign doing. But what about this seminary degree? What about my bills and debts? My calling conflicted with my career; my passions couldn't be a priority because they didn't bring profit.

Yet still I would observe others and become twisted with jealousy. Whether on TV or Facebook or in person, it seemed like there was a secret to life and nobody would share it with me. Some excelled at business; others lived vicariously for the gospel, traversing the globe with abandon Even with poverty and struggle, they seemed to be at peace with what they were doing, confident that they were in the center of their purpose.

Why couldn't I just give myself totally to business and be content? Or why couldn't there be a church, teaching, or preaching gig that paid enough to live on? Or why couldn't I be satisfied to live a simple countercultural life serving God with simplicity in rejection of any external recognition? No, I couldn't pick or choose just one. I wanted to find a way to have the best of both worlds.

So as I continued to stuff my anxieties and fears, my heart grew tougher and harder. I couldn't really blame God; that didn't seem logical. My undealt-with turmoil was becoming cancerous. Old and unhealthy patterns of coping resurfaced as new sinful habits sprouted as well. The resulting shame and guilt was a perfect fit to fill the gap of why life was stuck and barren.

Now all my attention was on me. I finally had a definite cause to blame for my results. I was the problem. I wasn't good enough. Not holy enough. My sins and weaknesses were creating bondage. I had opened a door and the enemy freely entered. He had a legal right (so I thought) to ensnare, curse, and torment me.

From this perspective, I would vacillate. Being a good Christian, I'd fight and resist staying down too long. I could easily find a verse in Romans to turn the tables and make myself feel forgiven or made new. So I would encourage myself and get back to work. Get back to asking, seeking, and knocking for the key solution. I knew somebody had it.

I read many books. Christian books, business books, motivational and personal development books. I listened to podcasts, watched sermons online, and TEDTalks. Eventually I came across real people. I found myself latching onto mentors, counselors, and pastors. I gleaned nuggets from successful people, old people, life coaches, and consultants. From free advice to paid and bartered advice, I dipped a little into every well I could find.

The interesting thing about meeting with people, as compared to reading the words penned by famous authors, was that none of them gave me simple steps for successful living. There were no secrets and no magic formulas. No one, even the super wealthy, had any easy answers. They all seemed to listen more than they spoke. And when they responded to my situation, they just gave simple and direct responses.

I was told things like:

> *I think you're doing fine and you just need to keep at it.*
>
> *Why are you looking to change what you're doing?*
>
> *God needs people with character, not talent. You are building your character. So just be patient and stay faithful.*
>
> *Don't you know God uses people in business just as much or more than those in the church?*
>
> *Why can't you bring all your gifts and talents into your work?*
>
> *God needs people like you in the world, not in the church.*

I always walked away slightly encouraged and slightly dissatisfied. Some of the ideas resonated, but some of it sounded like excuses and justifications. It seemed that people wanted me to settle or take a seat in the box of their worldview. It all had the appearance of wisdom, but no power to bring a conviction that I was exactly where I was destined to be.

Perhaps I was just closed off, not yet ready to hear what I needed. What I wanted was a guaranteed solution that would not cost me anything. I think it takes a bit of brokenness and desperation to step into something new. And for each person, the timeframe of breaking varies. In scripture, we see transformations take as little as three years for some and in others, as long as 40. Every person and each situation is unique. But as long as there is unrest, that feeling reveals that there is still a fight and germination of something yet to be born.

But not being ready, all I had was misguided zeal. I was, and still am, a young man, and what we tend to count on is our strength.

"I write to you, fathers, because you know him who is from the beginning. I write to you, young men, because you are strong..." 1 John 2:14

So to me doing something always trumped doing nothing. Have you heard the expression "You can't steer a parked car"? So though I didn't know what to do and I had no peace, I just did stuff in order to feel better. I helped with a church plant. I taught theology at a local college. I traveled to Africa to help train leaders. But it was all out of an orphan mentality. I was the prodigal son's big brother, active, obedient, jealous, and dissatisfied.

As a Christian who feels called to do great things for God, I crave participation in something major, something deep, something radical. I aspired for significance, felt I was special but also was stuck.

I've wanted to help others by sharing what I knew while hiding who I really was. But that's the picture I gained from many of the books I read. I heard stories of greatness and amazing exploits. Even in rags-to-riches stories, it seemed like when riches are obtained, the rags no longer exist.

Everyone magnifies their strengths and minimizes their weaknesses, their doubts, and even their luck. When we look with hindsight into our journey, we can see patterns and related coincidences. We can pull out principles and wisdom and turn them into tweetable phrases and how-to blog posts.

It all sounds and looks good to others, but what really matters is the condition of our souls within. Character really is critical. And character, i.e. the status of our soul, is measured in the present, not in comparison with our past, our future, or another person's.

When I became a Christian, and interpreted the teachings of scripture and preachers, my perspective was skewed and had set me up for disappointment. But by God's grace, and the wisdom obtained from persevering, my sorrow has turned to joy.

My dream in writing this book is for it to help you find freedom to live each day in the grace predetermined for your life.

I don't profess to be clever, but I do feel I have heard from God on a few subjects and possess a unique perspective. If you have been disappointed and let down on your journey, I hope that with these words you will be motivated to get back in the game and do what you were created to do.

# OVERVIEW

I write these words to you, my brothers and sisters. As fellow recipients of the grace of God, I admonish you to live a life worthy of the sacrifice paid for with the transformation of your soul. We have a responsibility–not to act perfectly nor to judge the world, but to bring a little bit of Heaven to Earth. We are ambassadors of another kingdom with territory to steward and reconcile with God.

But sometimes with the deep realities of our responsibility we become burdened and distracted. We experience consuming opportunities and unexpected loss. We have feelings, doubts, disappointments, and frustrations that cannot be wiped away with the phrase "in Jesus' name." No, we have to endure hardships, thorns in the flesh, and cares of the world.

I believe that everyone who has a call, a work, or responsibility needs to grasp this balance. When you have a talent and access to make something better, you will also receive a burden for that area. Your life will be measured not merely on your morality or spirituality, but on your stewardship of your territory.

In the few pages that comprise this book, I offer to you a perspective about life and God. I hope to save you a little bit of cyclical meandering by enlightening your view on certain limiting beliefs. Limited thinking will not only disappoint you; it can leave you wounded and discouraged. God is the most loving, pure, selfless, and generous being. But when you know Him partially, then experienced hurts or disappointments have the potential of inventing lies: lies about God, lies about yourself, or lies about other people.

Most of what I write is an attempt to expose partial truths which work for some, but not for others. When this happens, you can fall through the cracks and feel like a victim, and become stuck.

In order to move forward in God and in life, you need to get over any anger or bitterness about what you thought life *would be* like. Reflecting on all your would-haves and could-haves in the midst of God's healing truth can help you exchange ungodly beliefs for godly ones.

## *Personal Inventory*

A few years ago I felt I needed to stop and assess my beliefs. Because I had gone through so many sharp ups and downs in prior years, I wanted to reflect and see how my circumstances had influenced my beliefs.

I wish I could say that nothing changed. That my view of God, scripture, church, life, money, success, and purpose were unhindered by challenging events, but that is far from true. Most of my original beliefs were taught to me from pastors, teachers, TV, and books. Only a minority of my worldview was based on personal experience, scripture, and prayer.

As my life traversed outlier scenarios, I began to question what was really true. Have you ever stopped to think about what you believe? Like what you *really* believe? Not just what you've been told to believe, nor the facts that lay dormant in your head. But what life has taught you and what you actually live? It's like when people say, "Show me your checkbook or calendar and I'll show you what you really value." We may say this or that is important, but the way we consistently spend our hard-earned money and time will reveal a better picture of our values.

And so, what I did was write down my core beliefs about life, God, and other principles, and ideas. Some of the things I wrote down were:

> Seasons trump calling. We must learn to rest and trust in what God is doing, and not just what he said.

> Life and truth may be black and white to God, but for most of us, all we see are shades of gray. There are realities and situations wherein the Bible doesn't speak to us literally. Thus there must be a higher

form of faith or trust or wisdom for life.

I'm ok. Sins, deficiencies, weaknesses, or bad habits neither cancel nor delay God's will and timing. But the process of deliverance happens as He had always foreordained.

Christianity was never meant to be done or walked through alone. Close and trusting relationships are critical for every phase of the journey. Don't try to handle everything yourself. Don't try to handle most things on your own. Learn to rely less and less on yourself.

Lastly,

God views people without distinctions of *secular* or *sacred* but simply wants hearts to love Him fully. I must stop putting certain activities or people on pedestals and drop my own judgments about what I am doing or not doing.

I wrote down many other lessons, but for this book I've chosen six to share. If you can be grounded in the reality that God is always good and never let Him go, you can get through anything and become all He created you to be. God is better than we all imagine He could be. And now is the time to receive clarity and reignite faith.

## *Six Uncommon Lessons*

*Lessons 1–3: Seasons Trump Calling, Prioritizing Divine Purpose, Normalizing Failure*

The first three lessons are to help reorient us or reassess where we are. We have a glimpse about who we were made to be but our life has not emulated that glorious picture.

- Our calling will take time and we need to focus on the current season.

- We need to always prioritize God's purposes or divine purpose as we figure out our specific and unique design.

- Failure is not final, but often essential. If we can normalize failure, freely anticipate grace and mercy, we can move steadily from glory to glory.

*Lessons 4–6: Living with Ambiguities, Removing Limitations, Sanctified Ambition*

The second three lessons deal with the possibilities of what we can be or do or where we can go in His name.

- We not only reorient the present but we rethink the future.

- We break out of limited thinking and live by faith instead of sight.

- What is really possible to the soul devoted to God? If we invite God into every inch of our lives are there any limits to what He can do through us?

As Christians, we try to see life through the lenses of Biblical stories and scriptural principles. However, no matter how much knowledge we have, there remains a veil that limits us from full comprehension of our situations and stories.

Removing veils is the real purpose behind this book.

The six uncommon lessons are really there to give a new perspective that will help us move forward.

The title is *Sanctified Ambition* because this phrase implies the context necessary to embrace forward progress for the Christian. The lessons of the book are only relevant for the individual committed to walking with God and being a blessing to the world. Ambition is required to see the fulfillment of any worthwhile goal. It's necessary so we never bury our talents and succumb to setbacks. But refusing to divorce your faith and spiritual family and heavenly Father is even more important. A sanctified and ambitious Christian is one who knows God intimately, has their affections on Heaven's priorities, and manifests that though their service for people.

It has taken me years to be open to seeing the infinite variety of God's ways and wisdom. The book you are reading will open you up to seeing how God is faithful and can work beyond your imagination.

Let's get started!

# 1:
# SEASONS TRUMP CALLING

"To everything there is a season, and a time to every purpose under the Heaven." Ecc. 3:1

"God is faithful to both conceive and deliver." Arvell Craig

## *The Realization of Dreams*

It's only natural to dream. When the mind shuts down from the busyness of the day, it allows the unconscious to awake. The soul will explore and illuminate deep and often perplexing things. Likewise, when we escape present reality and imagine a preferable future, we revel in the possibilities of what our lives could become.

Whether awake or asleep, if we sense that our dream has come from God it changes our entire approach. When God shares with us His dream for our lives, we sense Him taking residence in our emptiness. Voids that we didn't know we had are flooded with life and light blazes across the caverns of our neglected soul. A word from God, written, spoken, or just realized, changes everything when applied specifically and personally to our life.

I wish someone told me after the God idea comes–via dream, prophecy, or imagination, there would be years of preparing and processing before I would see it realized. That in between sowing and reaping, planting and harvesting, there would be time… make that a LONG time. My prayer life felt like a resounding *are we there yet, are we there yet?* But no, I had a dream but no idea of what or how long it would take.

But it's not just about the time it takes to see a dream come true. The real tricky part is learning not to be so consumed with our perception of our dream that we miss the calling on the present. There is a day called *today*, filled with purpose and value and meaning, even though it may seem quite ordinary. Our journey towards the materialization of our calling or dream is filled with tiny moments called *todays*. In each of these todays, God is calling us to be present and alert and to work fully in whatever state we are in, as if we are already in the divine assignment.

This is the first principle or perspective I want to share. God's call on your life will always be subordinated to the current season you are in. You must discern the season and submit to it first as you navigate your way to your dream.

## *Seasons Trump Calling*

When your life is not manifesting fruit consistent with the seeds God planted in your heart, the problem may be the season. I know the initial response is more cultivation, more water, and more effort. But the ability to discern the season can save you tremendous strain and emotional pain. To work towards a God-given goal out of God's timing will bring an offended, rejected, and confused heart.

Receiving a God idea or calling is like having a personal North Star, always the brightest light amongst an abundance of competing ideas. It can be an unrelenting nudge in our hearts, whispering a contradicting message from that of our shift supervisor. That thing can be more important than the mundane responsibilities we're subjected to; however, the boring present cannot be ignored.

Looking into the Biblical biographies of Joseph, Moses, and David shows a common landscape of dreaming or calling–followed by one or a series not-yet seasons, and then the finally-it's-happening moment. In each of their situations, the not-yet season gave no indication that preparation was taking place. But as we view these stories in hindsight, we see that each purposeful detour was necessary to arrive prepared in the end.

## *Joseph*

Joseph was called to do great things. His calling was clearly presented in a dream and confirmed by future dreams. Yet in spite of the call on his life, in spite of his natural gifts and abilities present, God's path led him through a process of seasons. Joseph spent years working in realms completely foreign to his understanding of his dreams.

The gist of Joseph's dream showed him as an authority for his family. He was the second youngest of twelve sons, but in the night he saw a destiny of importance and influence. But Joseph's story didn't remain in the company of his family. His life ventured into foreign countries, in service and slavery to distant kings. But in every circumstance, Joseph gave his all to the circumstances in which he found himself. He seemed to embody the words of Paul, ". . . For I have learned in whatever state I am, to be content in it." Ph. 4:11.

## David

David was called to do great things. His early childhood wasn't anything special, and yet the prophet Samuel anointed him to be the king of the nation. What could be more dramatic and clear than the spiritual leader of the country pouring a bottle of oil over your head and commissioning you as the king!!

But the following days and years of David's life were not full of respect, royalty, and submission by all those around him. David had a call and he also had a season. His season as a son and little brother still had to be honored. When he became a musician in King Saul's household, that position required dedication. When he was a soldier in the army under Saul's authority that also mandated his complete obedience–even while he was anointed king.

I find David's life is encouraging because of the dramatic and blatant call on his life. Even with the clarity of his identity and purpose, it didn't make life go any easier. The journey was not much smoother than Joseph's. Whether your destiny is revealed with public fanfare or whispered while you sleep, you will have seasons in life that are not only for enduring, but for honoring and committing to fully.

The concept that seasons trump calling gave me freedom to know where to put my pent-up energy. We are not supposed to hold out our true self until we are fully recognized and independent. We need to give ourselves wholly to the season and circumstance we find ourselves in.

Colossians 3:23–24, "Work willingly at whatever you do, as though you were working for the Lord rather than for people. Remember that the Lord will give you an inheritance as your reward…"

## *Moses*

Moses was called to do great things. (Are you catching any theme yet?) His infancy was divinely preserved. His childhood was a privileged upbringing in the house of Pharaoh. He somehow sensed he was called to bring freedom to his captive relatives. He had direct access to Pharaoh, a burning conviction for justice, and yet his first attempt ended in dramatic failure.

Many people try for years to be in a situation as Moses. They try to network and hobnob around the right people who can help them achieve their goals. But even with so many things seemingly divinely arranged, he was still rejected by those he desired to help. Being out of season and ill prepared, he commits a felony and has to flee for his life. Forty years elapse before he rediscovers his dream.

Joseph was relegated to serving in captivity, David was tormented by a terrible boss, and Moses simply forsook all affiliation with his call. With each of these stories, the dream was clear and the in-between season was long and hard. And so, while living in the in-between, I've found it helpful to ask myself, *what season am I in?* I know what God said. I know what I dream of doing. But right now, there are demands on my time and attention that cannot be ignored.

My children are in need of a father. Not just a provider and physical presence, but a personal, affectionate leader and cultivator to make sure they grow up with Christ's character. My school loans and mortgage want a piece of my paycheck. My wife wants my attention. Many things require faithfulness and commitment. No, it doesn't look like getting a second job will help me change the world, but perhaps it will bring down the weight of debt hanging over me.

*Seasons Trump Calling* is a perspective to help us live full of trust and faith today. God requires us to be present to the present. He says not to worry about tomorrow. Don't invite tomorrow's responsibilities onto today's to-do list. As one author put it, "Don't time travel." That creates unnecessary stress and anxiety that we have no capacity or provision for handling.

For most of us, we are not living in the reality of our call. At least not according to how we presume it to be. And so we are instructed, "Do not say tomorrow this or that is going to happen." (James 4:13-14) Like Joseph's arrogance, "Tomorrow you're all going to bow down to me!" No, you don't even know what will happen this evening. All you know is that God's will is going to happen.

I believe that the scripture that tells us we must be faithful over the little things, in order to be ruler of much, refers to how we live in the not-yet, the in-between. God whispers his dreams to us, but he doesn't command us to make them happen. He calls us to greatness and then leads us on a journey to discover how great He can be when we learn to work with Him.

Oh how I wish someone told me, maybe as a rule of thumb, anticipate a twenty-year process like Joseph, a thirty-year process like Jesus, or a forty-year process like Moses. Then I would try to live my life as a marathon of faithful endurance and commitment while maintaining intimacy.

I wish someone told me that I did not have to make God's seed in me grow. That I couldn't make it happen. Instead of living in the clouds, my calling was to live as faithful steward of what was presently entrusted to me.

Stop worrying about your call. God is faithful to both conceive and deliver. Commit to the season you are in. Keep your dreams in sight, but don't let it block you from treating today like an indispensable gift.

## 2:
## DIVINE PURPOSE

"Begin with the end in mind." Stephen Covey

"The greatest tragedy in life is not death, but a life without a purpose." Myles Munroe

I remember the first time I met with Dave. As I strolled into Panera Bread a little after 7 am, there he was waiting for me in a booth. It was much earlier than I've ever met with anyone and I was glad I was only a few minutes late. He was gracious about my tardiness and we immediately started to talk casually.

Eventually Dave pulled out a piece of paper and began to explain to me what he called "general purpose." He said that before we can start talking about God's unique purpose for my life that I first had to understand God's general purpose. General purpose was kind of like God's foundational blueprint for all humanity. It was a way of understanding what every human being was made for. It made no difference whether or not one could become the greatest sports star or spiritual miracle worker. If they didn't understand general purpose, all would be done in vain.

Dave laid out for me how it is that we know God and know what he wants from us in the most general sense. That, of course, is the Bible and the church or community of people who follow the ways of Jesus. Within the scriptures, we learn principles and commandments. We see in the life of Jesus the most illustrative presentation of God's nature: His love and His compassion, His selflessness and creativity to solve problems and meet the needs of people. We also see in Jesus anger at the Devil and with sorrow towards people who are lost or in pain.

Jesus also had a *pissed-off-ness* for people who created barriers and non-essential rules to come to God.

Dave told me that first day, with all we see in Jesus and the scriptures, those of us who truly understand and bask in the intimacy of communing with Him will begin to change. He said the key to life begins and ends with abiding with Christ. Within Jesus Christ is the answer and satisfaction of the soul. He has an eternity of endless love and joy that is not only experienced in Heaven but can be sampled here on Earth.

General purpose was explained to me as knowing who I am, not as a unique and distinct creation, but as a beloved son. As a child of God, it is my responsibility and privilege to abide and represent the nature, kingdom, and heart of God.

Dave was first trying to get me to understand that no matter what was happening in life, whichever season I was in the midst of, I needed to abide with Christ. I also needed to take care of my wife and daughter. These were priorities that should never be questioned, and never should be neglected.

If I am responsible for the stewardship of my family, I of course would always need to work, and not just work to survive or make the minimum necessary. Rather, I needed to make more than enough. I was to love my wife as Christ loved the church, even giving Himself for it. I would not likely have to sacrifice my life for my family, but my own time and needs may often take a backseat to their comfort and security.

This is divine purpose, a purpose that is foundational and relevant to all. As the Bible teaches, and as we discern for ourselves, there are some things we just do. We don't have to fear and we don't have to pray about everything. We know we should not steal and kill. But we also know we must make money. Sure, we can pray about which opportunity is the best. However, when all is said and done, even if we don't have a clear direction, we still have to decide.

I love this concept of purpose because it's like a rock. It's steady. It's safe. When I'm not feeling super spiritual or adventurous to take on new things, when I don't know what to do and I feel like God isn't directing me, I can trust in my understanding of His love and nature. He's like a Father. He is a Father! He knows my end from my beginning and actually exists in both places!

I do believe that each of us is unique and we should seek to go deeper into our specific calling. However, a more sure foundation is knowing God's ways, understanding and living totally aligned with his divine purpose.

In this process of abiding in Christ daily, we can't help but become stirred. We will eventually be unsatisfied. As Paul says in Philippian 2:13, "For it is God who works in you, both to will and to work for His good pleasure."

God will nudge on our will and desires. He will prompt us to seek deeper impact. This is different from simply wanting to be famous or aspiring for success. This is spiritual significance and a hunger to align our DNA to glorify God. We long to interconnect Heaven and Earth. When Christian values, spiritual convictions, and natural abilities come together, we start to sense our sweet spot.

But it does not come quickly. God has a plan and process that we must journey through.

Prophetic awareness doesn't speed the gestation period between revelation and manifestation. Patience and long-suffering are fruit of the spirit for a reason. They are not optional attributes, but requirements for all who seek to live spiritually significant and purposeful lives.

And God is faithful.

But can you and I trust in his faithfulness?

"I would rather die trusting God than live in unbelief." - Smith Wigglesworth

I have spent much of my Christian life trying to make God's will and purpose come to pass in my life. God gave me a glimpse of my calling but He only stirred in a desire for Himself. Instead of continually feasting on Him, I hungered to be used by and for Him. I have been double-minded for too many years because of lack of trust in His faithfulness.

God is so amazing, that He not only wants the best for us, He Himself becomes the fuel and drive to do the things that please Him. He makes Himself the author and finisher, the beginning and end. We are in the middle. We are stewards and ambassadors, tools and instruments, beautifully crafted to do good works.

We have the freedom to enjoy the fruits of our labor, enjoy our spouses and children, and eat freely of the fruit of the land. We are no longer bound by external laws, but guided by the Holy Spirit from within.

## RESOURCE

Purpose is a powerful subject and it does get specific. Each person is unique. Embracing your uniqueness is a power in and of itself. Discovering your unique purpose is a book unto itself, and I'm not attempting to speak on it now. However, I do want to make a referral.

For maybe five years, I've been involved in, taught, and coached in a certain methodology. It's called Your One Degree. This program is comprehensive and builds upon the foundation of a Christian who is established in and committed in their faith.

The life of a Christian begins by establishing a foundation of Godly character. We learn from scripture, pastors, and the church how to live. We gain a new language and disciplines like prayer and worship and meditation. From here God adapts our mind and then transforms our heart. His Spirit on the inside is given access and permission to develop our born-again spirit.

As the Your One Degree program teaches, many of us will develop a holy unrest. We become unable to simply go through the motions of life, personal, occupational, or ministry. It's like a wall has been raised and though we may fight it, we cannot break through living life as usual. If you are not counseled or coached properly, men or women will fall into temptation or addictions trying to fill their emptiness. Others will try to perform more, do church more, ministry, or pray more, and yet this will not satisfy.

In this stalemate of the soul, if we are not living our lives in line with our sweet spot or unique purpose, nothing else will do. It seems God brings us into this kingdom, into His family and changes our affections and appetites. As we seek Him more, He helps us to shift and seek for our true calling by restraining us from going through the motions.

Yes, purpose is really a huge subject. If you've found yourself in this place of unrest, here's how you can learn more. Visit YourOneDegree.com. Let Dave know you learned about it here. He or someone else will guide you towards gaining clarity and discovering, as they call it, "your one degree."

Note: The program is completely free and I gain nothing by mentioning it. I am a coach with the program, but I'm not suggesting you work with me. I do encourage you to consider looking over the website to better understand it. It has helped me and thousands of others. Again, visit YourOneDegree.com for details.

# 3:
# NORMALIZING FAILURE

"Every adversity, every failure, every heartache carries with it the seed of an equal or greater benefit." Napoleon Hill

"For though the righteous fall seven times, they rise again…" Proverbs 24:16

After I finished my speech, there wasn't much applause. In fact, only one person came up to me afterward to chat with me about my talk. I was asked to speak to a group of students at the local university. The directions were to share about my life with God. Perhaps I should have talked about something more uplifting. Some amazing turnaround that God had done, some healing, or dramatic deliverance. People love hearing rags-to-riches stories with emotionally gripping close calls showing off God's power and love for those who turn their lives over to Him.

Unfortunately I didn't have any personal stories like that. I figured I would do best if I spoke on something I had a lot of experience with.

I talked about failure.

My experience with failure was extensive and I hoped that I could be an encouragement. But as it turns out, this group of ambitious and astute private university students couldn't really relate to my story—at least not yet, at least not publicly.

Failure is such a drag to talk about, but for me it needs to be a part of the conversation. Whether you are talking about life, love, business, or success, failure is a natural companion. Those who do not experience failure are often those who don't experience anything new. Nothing new and not much growth either.

Depending on how you view them, past failures can demoralize or immobilize you. They can become a fixture of weakness and brokenness creating a psychological limp. Without a strong mental and emotional core, you will not be able to aim high or fight through obstacles that are sure to come against you. Failure, if not appropriately dealt with, becomes deadly.

The ways we approach potential failure or reflect on past failure is essential to the way we live, trust, and see ourselves. It can color our identity, come up as we compare ourselves to others, our hopes and potentials. But worst of all it can plague us spiritually in whether we approach God in confidence or apprehension.

Failure is either a flat tire on the road to success or a detour on the path of perfection. Your perspective determines whether it's a speed bump or a mile marker, a tollbooth or traffic citation. Based on that view, your response can be indifferent, fueled, or downcast.

In my six years of undergraduate studies, I failed to make the passing grade over 20 times. I had to repeat most of my early math, physics, and engineering courses a couple of times each. This could have been taken as intellectual defeat, but for me, I looked at it differently. I was in a challenging major and many people who came before me struggled to complete the classes on their first time was well.

Because of my knowledge of the norm, I didn't take the defeat personally. Even more, I discovered through my struggle that I had talent for teaching and tutoring. After I finally passed the courses, I helped younger students avoid the failures I endured.

There is a concept here that I think will help you if you've ever struggled repeatedly to overcome something.

If you start asking other people to discover their experiences, you will realize failure is much more common than you think. Peers may not want to admit all their struggles, but if you ask someone 10 or 20 years your senior, you'll find them more open and honest.

After seeing the downturns of others, you will see your failures as normal. I would hope you won't justify or make excuses for them, but you mustn't live with condemnation. Failure can create shame and isolation. This will leave you alone with your negative thoughts with no perspective.

If you cannot find anyone to share with you their personal battles and failures, you could start reading biographies. It doesn't matter what type you read, be it about a politician, entertainer, business person, or whatever. Failure is much more a part of the story of living with ambition and achievement than many admit.

The goal here is normalizing failure, and even expecting it. I believe having a healthy and realistic expectation will cause the journey to be much more endurable. If you think because you're a Christian, or because you've prayed, or because you know your calling that you can avoid struggles, breakdowns or mishaps, you'll be shocked and gravely disappointed.

I vividly recall a story when I first read the classic financial book, *Rich Dad, Poor Dad*. In one of the early chapters, the author Robert Kiyosaki relates how he learned the average millionaire fails or goes bankrupt eight to ten times before arriving at success. This realization was something that the author knew before he even started his first business. Therefore, he was prepared to persevere through hard times before he arrived at his ultimate destination.

How many of us expect to fail or anticipate the need for perseverance. Whether it's in business, or selecting our vocation, finding a spouse, or living a holy life, we need to be prepared to accept storms as natural events. But what happens when you don't have this mindset? How do you chart a course that avoids turbulence, risk, and insecurity?

Years ago, I read a book called *Failing Forward*. Inside, author John Maxwell gives page after page of stories that illustrate the reality and necessity of failure. Inside, there was one poem that reminded me of some people I knew and I desperately wanted to avoid becoming. I hope these forty-two words bring conviction to you like they did to me.

> "There was once a very cautious man, who never laughed or played.
>
> Never risked, never tried, never sang or prayed.
>
> And when one day he passed away, his insurance was denied.

For since he never really lived, they claimed he never died."

-- John Maxwell, *Failing Forward*

Here are three takeaways for you to hold on to as you pursue your ambitions and deal with hardships and setbacks.

1. Normalize failure, i.e. renounce the idea of perfection. Failure is not a bad word, it's not an anomaly. It's a part of the learning process towards any worthwhile endeavor.

They say Babe Ruth was the strikeout king, but no one talks about that. His willingness to endure striking out is what also allowed him to become the homerun king.

2. If you have struggled and overcome an issue, you become qualified to help others get over that problem. That is, if you are open and honest about it.

Those who've endured a struggle and fought through are often the best tutors, counselors, and encouragers. No one wants to follow or listen to someone who's never failed. We don't identify or feel comfortable divulging our issues with a perfectionist. We may ask them for help or advice, but we won't go into details of our true state.

Allow your failures to be testimonies of God's goodness and grace. In spite of whatever setbacks you have come through, you haven't given up. That is something to be proud of. It is something that will lift someone else who is in the middle or beginning of their own struggle. They need to hear that real people have problems and have overcome them.

3. As you look to the future, let not your past failures cause you to aim low. Don't aim low or think down about yourself. The way you see yourself directly relates to how you approach your future. If you have normalized failure, then you should see greatness is still possible.

"If you aim at nothing, you will hit it every time." -- Zig Ziglar

Dietrich Bonhoeffer, the German theologian, pastor, and martyr said, "One must be more passionate to obey God, than to avoid sin."

The key here is to always keep your eyes fixed on your God and your goal. Looking at others, or even looking to yourself, can be a distraction and detriment. The spiritual provisions and talent and grace that God provides for you are not outside the confines of slipups and mistakes. They include them.

"To them that love God, all things work together for good, even sin" – St. Augustine.

## RESOURCE

Have you ever heard of Celebrate Recovery? Celebrate Recovery is a ministry that is available in churches worldwide for helping people to recover from personal struggles or addictions of any kind. They meet weekly and provide an open and safe place to hear how others have learned to trust Christ with their problems. If you desire, you can share your struggles in a small group or you can commit to a yearlong 12-step program, based on the beatitudes.

The reason I bring up Celebrate Recovery is that it is an opportunity for you to sit in the company of other men or women and get a powerful picture of what grace looks like and how it works to restore and heal. You could be in the presence of business leaders and the homeless; people who've trashed their lives but yet are looking to Jesus to turn it around for good.

The environment of Celebrate Recovery can help you get a realistic picture of what life is like beyond the masks most people wear. It can also help you get over yourself and come to grips with your total need for God's love and power to help you become who He intends you to be.

To learn more or to find a local gathering, visit: www.CelebrateRecovery.com

# 4:
# REMOVING LIMITATIONS

There are more options for living in God's will than we normally perceive. The application of our calling or purpose reaches further and deeper than the simple boxes we try to put them in.

The key is realizing that God values every activity equally when it's done for His glory.

Colossians 3:17 says, "And whatever you do or say, do it as a representative of the Lord Jesus, giving thanks through him to God the Father."

I used to put a label on occupations or activities as sacred or spiritual, and then on others as secular or worldly. With that mindset, I placed higher emphasis on certain things and a lower value on others. Personally, I wanted to make tangible impact in the world for God—not just for *good*, but the way I labeled activities inappropriately discriminated against them.

The way we compartmentalize God will, in effect, put limitations on ourselves. God is so big and so all encompassing—he wants to remove the excuses and limitations that we place on Him and ourselves. With each distinction, label, and category, we dish out judgment or self-righteousness.

We put people on pedestals and see ourselves as grasshoppers. We may think so-and-so is more gifted or less sinful and reason that's why they have achieved success. But God chooses and uses weak and broken people to confound the wise and strong.

Though I'm not completely free from this narrow way of thinking, I have taken major strides in the direction of better recognizing how

God indiscriminately uses people from all walks of life.

Let me share a story that helped chip away my old mindset.

In my introduction, I described how 2007 was a hallmark year in my world. But, for the university that I had just graduated from, their story had hit a cataclysmic low.

In the fall of that year, accusations of sexual and financial impropriety hit the local news and soon made its way to national attention. Students, alumni, and Christians worldwide would be following the controversy and scandal for weeks. Amidst the developing allegations, the school's 45 million dollars of debt, and 60 million dollars of critical maintenance was uncovered and posed an imminent threat to the school's existence.

Fast forward 18 months.

I'm sitting inside a packed meeting room at a local Italian restaurant. I, along with other university alumni, am hearing the behind-the-scenes details of the miracle turnaround our beloved alma mater had experienced during the darkest period of its history.

The speaker was a billionaire businessman named Mart. I knew of his name only from the news. He and his family came to the rescue, donating tens of millions to the university and orchestrating changes that would secure a healthy foundation for the school's now promising future.

His behind-the-scenes story sheds even greater light on how desperate the situation really was and how miraculous the intervention of God was.

Mart and his family, like many other Christians, watched the news and learned of the nightmare situation. And instead of allowing their heads to be consumed with judgment and criticism, their hearts were broken as they thought of the needs of the students.

Mart described how the scandals of televangelists in the 1980s were devastating to people worldwide and not just those directly employed. Similarly, the downfall of my university would not only affect its students, but Christian universities and believers around the world.

With that realization, they called a family meeting, bringing together five couples, and considered investing a large portion of their family fortune into a school with which they personally had no ties or affiliations.

With fasting, praying, and discussions, they decided to give a donation over five times larger than they had ever given in the past.

Upon hearing this, hair across my arms stood and goose bumps flooded my flesh. I was hearing firsthand of an impossible miracle turnaround that was beyond my imagination.

What most saw as controversy and shame, these people looked upon with eyes of compassion as they sought restoration over judgment.

Who were these people and how could they give so much with seemingly nothing to gain?

What I normally thought could impact the world for the Kingdom was being expanded. Yes, they were Christians and had Christian businesses, but to me that didn't necessarily mean you're operating differently from any other company.

Businesses run on economic principles and investments are made based on the ROI and the stability of the organization. But fasting and praying as family before making decisions? Wasn't that only for pastors, evangelists, and missionaries?

Again, I'm really not that ignorant. I know God uses all people. But I still saw the more spiritual, Bible-talking vocations with a little bit more reverence.

But in this scenario, one family of Christian businesspeople impacted more lives than ten thousand typical ministers or preachers.

Witnessing this story disrupted the compartmentalizing boxes that I've had for business and ministry. I've had to endure my business activities while believing that my work for Christ happens only when quoting scriptures or standing in a pulpit.

When the majority of my efforts were for providing for my family's material needs, I would suffer from what I called "ministry guilt," the feeling that I needed to do some type of church-related work to count for God.

I would travel to Africa and teach theology in local colleges in order to feel like I was doing something that mattered. I needed something to say to people when asked what I was doing with my seminary degree.

Just the other day I was talking with a guy at Starbucks and I asked him, "What do you do?"

He unenthusiastically told me he was a hotel bellman but then quickly explained his real passion was building relationships with local Muslims. I related instantly to his identity conundrum.

He did one thing for money and did something else as a passion or ministry. One for God and one for…self?

In the book, *Quitter: Closing the Gap between Your Day Job and Your Dream Job*, author Jon Acuff talks about this creatively. In his writing, he calls it the "I'm/But Generation," as in "I'm a _____, but I want to be a _____."

We could all fill in the blanks with a number of things.

Most people are not doing what they wish they were doing. My only concern is when we devalue what we're doing inappropriately. When we devalue what we do, we stifle what we can hear from God, not allowing Him to partner with us.

"Whatever you do, work at it with all your heart, as working for the Lord, not for men," Col. 3:23.

If we do everything as if it's for the Lord, how can we think certain tasks or people are more valuable or important?

The same could be said about marriage and child rearing. There's nothing special or eternally vital about that, right?

Tell that to Esther.

Do you remember her story?

Here's the verse where she was confronted with whether or not she would take her seemingly practical, familial position lightly or yield it to God. She was lucky that she had a trusted cousin speak these words to her:

"For if you remain completely silent at this time, relief and deliverance will arise for the Jews from another place, but you and your father's house will perish. Yet who knows whether you have come to the kingdom for such a time as this?" (Esther 4:14 NKJV)

Esther was simply being beautiful and getting married. Yet these seemingly worldly or carnal values positioned her to be used by God to help save an entire nation.

When we box things and label them as *Godly* or *ministry* and see other areas differently, we're compartmentalizing God.

Carnality or worldliness is best used when describing our motives, not the specific activity.

Jesus once said that many people who perform amazing spiritual feats would be rejected from his Kingdom because they never really knew him.

Some put God in a box; others revere certain callings or look down on their lives because it isn't glamorous. I see all these as manifestations of the same root problem.

We see separations, levels, and distinctions in God, when we are all loved and valued the same. God has no caste system.

When we aspire to be our best for God, we need to accept who God made us and know that he loves everyone the same. We need to see God in every believer to the same degree.

We need to trust in every season that we have the ability to glorify God if we yield to him, as he leads. Most days aren't glamorous. Possibly, most years aren't special either. But faithfulness and openness will put us in the right place at the right time. And who we've become in God will be enough.

Let's remove the limits we place on ourselves and enjoy God enjoying us in everything we do.

# 5:
# LIVING WITH AMBIGUITIES

"For now we see through a glass, darkly; but then face to face: now I know in part; but then shall I know even as also I am known." - Paul the Apostle (1 Cor. 13:12)

"Life and truth maybe black and white to God, but for the rest of us, all we can perceive are shades of gray." - Arvell Craig

## *FUZZY LOGIC*

When I was a computer science student studying artificial intelligence, my professor introduced us to a concept called *fuzzy logic*. According to Wikipedia, *fuzzy logic* is a form of programming logic that deals with approximates rather than fixed results. In other words, it's a method for reaching a conclusion using partial ideas and best guesses.

Fuzzy logic is a contrast to traditional or binary logic that says there is only one acceptable answer for any given question. With fuzzy logic, the possibilities of response went beyond yes/no or multiple choice answers, but now had approximates. Call it fractions, ratios, real numbers, or decimals, the fact of the matter is between 0 and 1 exists an infinite number of possibilities.

For a computer to have human-like intelligence, not just stored answer data, it had to be able process situations with more than right-or-wrong, yes-or-no answers. It needed fuzzy logic programmed into it. You see, no matter how much information was stored inside a computer, it still could not outperform humans.

This same shift in perspective is necessary for Christian maturity, a shift from a binary, black/white based approach into an evolving, deepening, or flexible reasoning. Simply storing more and more information will not help you solve complex personal problems. Likewise, seeking after more and more knowledge will be a vain pursuit for steering your life.

Fulfilling your life's purpose and finding satisfaction will not come from approaching life like solving a multiple-choice exam. A well-lived life is more like answering an essay or oral exam. It's subjective to the heart of the individual and the nature of God.

As children we are taught a foundational level of knowledge from our schools and parents. As spiritual children, we are taught from pastors and church leaders Biblical principles of salvation, morality, ethics, and stewardship. All this information, natural or spiritual, is helpful but also elementary.

In Galatians 3, Paul describes Biblical laws as a temporary tutor escorting us into a relationship with Christ. This is a change from law to grace, or from sight to faith or the letter to the Spirit. It's a change from words written on tablets to the living logos engrafted on our heart.

Unfortunately this style of thinking and living is not common. We are taught to use the Bible as an instruction manual, not as an invitation for encounters and fellowship with the living Word. I know some use the acronym B.I.B.L.E as in **B**asic **I**nstructions **B**efore **L**eaving **E**arth, but in my life, I constantly come across situations and circumstances that go beyond the basics...

When I spent years searching through books and mentors for some secret strategy for figuring life out, I was acting as if the world operated in a logical, black or white manner. If my situation wasn't going the right way, the problem was simply a lack of information. And with the right information applied and lived, success should be guaranteed, right?

A major breakthrough happened for me when I started becoming friends with pastors. For the first time, my interaction wasn't based on being counseled by them, nor was I being hired to build a website or marketing campaign. No, these friendships were Christ-centered with mutual accountability, confession, and understanding. In this intimate setting, I began hearing about the struggles and problems they had in their churches, homes, or personal lives. And I was astonished.

The first level of astonishment was that they were not super-spiritual nor were they zest-fully clean. In many ways they were like me and had struggles in various areas, and yet they were still faithfully serving their congregations. I always felt people's success or leadership came after moral weakness or character flaws were cleaned up or fixed. But these guys were not yet perfect.

The next thing that shocked me was that some pastors would occasionally drink alcohol or smoke a cigar–at times for evangelistic purposes, "becoming all things to all men. . ." But there were other times when it was just for enjoyment! Then, there were others who didn't believe in the law of tithing and yet their paychecks came from church tithes!? When I became a Christian, it was expressly drilled into me how there were certain activities–a/k/a "worldly" behaviors–that Christians just did not do. Or there were spiritual laws that necessitated blessing and prosperity.

Now let me clear something up for you. I'm not here to say I agree or disagree with anything these individuals did. I don't want to state a Biblical view on any particular issue. But what I hope to express is how my box, my black/white worldview, which was strict, fixed, and intolerant began to get a little... fuzzy.

I thought I had a grasp of what initiated God's blessing or disapproval. But when I started to gain insider knowledge of the lives of others, my false foundations and weak walls started to crumble. As I mentioned in the prologue, a first layer of disruption happened when my own life didn't go as I thought it would. Now, I was walking alongside people who had what I thought I wanted, and their situation didn't fit what I thought precipitated it. And so neither my self-condemnation nor judgments were justified.

Note: I never stopped believing in God nor did I ever question my salvation. But much of everything else that pertained to life and godliness, blessings or curses was now up for discussion.

So what about you?

Your situation, your convictions, your rules or beliefs, your life events will be completely different. But depending on the boxes you've created, the rules you use to govern your life–based on your opinion of scripture or what you were taught by another–will all be tested.

"Now if any man builds on the foundation with gold, silver, precious stones, wood, hay, straw, each man's work will become evident; for the day will show it because it is to be revealed with fire, and the fire itself will test the quality of each man's work." - 1 Cor. 3:12–13

I know what I've shared is challenging, but I encourage you to pray and reflect on this statement: "Life and truth may be black and white to God, but for us, all we can perceive are shades of gray."

The goal of this principle is to loosen your grip on the myriads of nonessential ideas that you've heard. Your facts and your knowledge are only a part of the story. Your expectations based on certain beliefs can either offend or disrupt your faith. Or you can learn, adjust, drop the nonessentials, and continue moving forward.

You only see in part, and the future will send you twists and curves that you won't be prepared for. But if you're flexible and open to looking in between the black and the white, you can discover beauty in shades of gray.

King Solomon, the wisest man who ever lived, said the fear of the Lord is the beginning of wisdom. He recognized that wisdom didn't begin with information, principles, or knowledge. Rather, it requires a posture of reverence and humility to God, Creator of Heaven and sustainer of all life on Earth.

When I think of what it means to fear God, the essence is realizing God is God and I am not. I also acknowledge that God knows everything, but I know only a very small part. Take the Apostle Paul, who encountered Jesus, had angelic visitations, and was taken up to Heaven and yet, he said, he only knew in part. How is it that we can think, even with our Bible and concordances, that we have all the answers?

The greatest scholar, plus the entire history of church tradition, plus our greatest sense of spirit-led clarity will all add up to be good, but never perfect. Do you think God expects us to have everything under control, placed neatly in predetermined containers labeled with every ingredient with their nutritional value? Yeah, I use to think the same way.

If you are a seeker of truth, you may eventually end up with one of two conclusions:

1. There is no truth! Nobody knows it all, thus you can't trust anyone! God can't even be trusted since all we know of Him was revealed from sinful and questionable people.

2. There is no perfect understanding of truth. Nobody on Earth knows it all, thus I have to trust God for all the things I can't guarantee. I guess I even have to trust sinful, weak, and broken people.

We all see through a glass darkly. This applies not only for deep intuitions regarding the future, controversial topics, or the sovereign will of God. It applies to much of what we think we know.

Within every reality, there is more than meets the eye. In every fact, our perspective is only a sliver of the full picture that God sees. When we realize this, it can free us from the pride, control, rebellion, and the judgment we place on ourselves and others.

This principle is a shift… to learn to live with ambiguities. Perhaps this is what it means to live by faith?

Life and truth may be black and white to God, but for the rest of us, all we can perceive are shades of gray.

.

# 6:
# SANCTIFIED AMBITION

"God speaks through gifts and abilities. If you are not sure of your purpose in life, just do what you are good at–it's God's gift to you." Joyce Meyer

"I think the biggest thing most of us need to surrender to God is our fear of the unknown and control of the known. We distance ourselves from true intimacy under the guise of holding onto our dreams and goals performed our way." - Arvell Craig

A few years ago I got the crazy idea to attempt to run a marathon. This was neither a dream nor a bucket list item. And I didn't have any real experience in running. What I did have was a strong dissatisfaction about life. My business kept me busy but I was unfulfilled. Technology was changing so fast that I couldn't keep up. I was falling behind and I had no extra energy to follow the details of what the future was turning into.

As a result I did like Forest Gump, and ran.

For the first few weeks I was running about three to four miles a day. After some time I decided to sign up for a popular local race. I had no goals regarding a certain speed or time, but I was just enjoying this new hobby. A few days before I officially signed up, an acquaintance called me a punk for only doing the 5K distance and challenged me to do the 15K. I didn't feel ready for such a distance, but was excited about the challenge, so I gave in.

The race, though difficult at times, was very enjoyable. Immediately I started looking for the next challenge. After about a month of searching and continued running, I signed up for a full 26.2 mile marathon.

The process of training for a full marathon was a life-changing experience. Six days a week I was given specific instructions on what I had to do to develop my body adequately for running four and a half hours nonstop. The daily regimen of instructions gave me hope that if I just followed the plan I would be ok.

More than that, it was turning me into another person, a person of commitment, dedication, and discipline. All those characteristics I knew were important and yet never stuck with me in the past with such consistency. And then, somewhere around the 10th or 12th week, I was hit with feelings of utter condemnation.

Why was I so committed to running and training for a marathon? How could I commit to something as meaningless and not be as committed to other areas? Regarding prayer, work, or even family time, I was a bit more lackadaisical. They had ebbs and flows and no schedule. But running... oh no, there were no options, never a plan B. Once I decided to train for a race, I always put in my daily miles. If I was as committed to work or prayer as I had been to running, who knows where I would be? The more I thought about this, the more I began feeling ashamed with my lack of priority.

One day I shared my feelings with my pastor. I was conflicted with my new passion and its contrast against the lackluster performance in other areas. I had drawn an illustration of the various areas of my life: spiritual, family, personal, dreams, and work. I was in the middle and yet there were these five extensions and values that I had in my life. All of which required time and attention, devotion, and commitment. But no matter how hard I tried, I'd never given them equal energy. There were always multiple areas lacking in what I felt necessary.

My pastor responded with a simple idea he termed *sanctified ambitions*. He told me the only thing I needed to do was to make sure that in every area Jesus was invited and glorified. He shared with me that, even in "spiritual" endeavors, we can go about them with the wrong motives and misguided intentions.

He told me, it doesn't matter what we are doing, be that spending intimate time with a spouse, or training for a marathon, or praying for the sick. The key is actively inviting Jesus into everything, and then become responsive to anything we sense that He may want.

There is no condemnation for those who are in Christ Jesus. There is no guilt or shame when Jesus is a present reality, a companion, and Lord. And that is what the Lord wants. The Lord desires fellowship with his children. Is there anything we can't invite Him to? Is there anywhere He won't go? No, I don't think it's possible.

When we invite the Lord to speak into any area of our lives and any concern of our hearts, we stay in perfect peace. When we have His peace, we can be sure that there is nothing to worry about.

Sanctifying our ambitions will apply to any and every sphere of life. To pursue financial success or a certain status in the world of music, movies, science, or education, it's all good to God. He actually desires that his people would not be mediocre, passive, or lethargic. God desires to give us the longings of our hearts. It is in our yearnings that He plants the seeds of greatness and gifts.

I used to wonder what makes the great great. How is it that certain people can achieve great exploits while the rest merely survive. There are many reasons for this and a great number of books are already written about it. When I investigated the behind-the-scenes activity, it included talent and hard work, but went deeper.

The gifting of God was not just in the talent or the skill, but the deep-rooted drive and desire that fuels relentless commitment. God seemed to put in their nature a gene for perseverance in a certain area of interest. He speaks and leads and prompts through the seeds of desire.

When you can recognize and appreciate this, you can be free to invite the Lord into your desires. Ps. 37:4: "Delight yourself in the LORD, and He will give you the desires of your heart." Do not fear that you must crucify your desires on the altar of spiritual service.

Romans 12:1 says your spiritual act of worship is presenting everything you have and everything you are to Him while you are living it. You are not sacrificing but presenting; you are choosing to expose every part of your soul to Him without reservation.

The ultimate sacrifice God requires was performed by Jesus on the cross. We are living sacrifices, like Abraham offering Isaac to the Lord. But unlike Abraham, we know the nature of God and we know that he isn't asking us to give up our most valuable possessions permanently. Our foundational interactions with God are that of father and son, daddy and daughter. As a father, His pleasure is seeing His children operate in healthy ways, using what He put in them and glorifying Jesus. As long as we abide by those simple constraints we have more freedom and more permission than we could ever imagine.

"When you're passionate about God you can trust your passions." - Erwin McManus

# EPILOGUE

"Now there were four men with leprosy at the entrance of the city gate. They said to each other, 'Why stay here until we die? If we say we'll go into the city—the famine is there, and we will die. And if we stay here, we will die. So let's go over to the camp of the Arameans and surrender. If they spare us, we live; if they kill us, then we die'." 2 Kings 7:3–4

The depression that weighed on the city of Samaria was insurmountable. Not only was there a fierce standoff with an enemy stronger and more equipped. Weeks had gone without supplies of food. Four lepers, outcasts by any account, were hanging out near the enemies' camp discussing their next steps. Their conversation didn't involve complaining or agonizing about the apparent lack of food or comfort. Their lives had undoubtedly been hard for a long time. The famine that hit their city was the last straw.

Standing on rock bottom gives tremendous perspective–all you can do is look up. Desperation is an understatement to describe what prompted these lepers to walk their disfigured and detestable bodies into the enemy's camp. But nevertheless, as the story goes, they said to one other, "Why stay here until we die?" Speaking of death was not language of negative confession, but rather an honest description of reality. And so, they entered into a place of speeding up destiny. That day, from either death or divine provision, they would meet their maker.

There is a saying that goes: "When the pain of change is less than the pain of remaining the same, only then will we take courageous action."

I can identify with those four lepers and I am thankful for the sovereignty of God. At times he allows us to enter into circumstances where making a hard decision isn't as hard as we thought.

My story was one of wasting away in an infinite wait. Disappointment and failure had shaken me to the core. Years went by and I lived off rotten manna and borrowed lampstand oil. I desperately wanted God to move supernaturally and remove all uncertainty. And so, I waited and waited, but he seemed to remain silent. Eventually there came a succession of clues. Pastors, dreams, and even strangers began to give hints that God was in the process of doing something. My excitement grew but my feet remained still. My eyes surveyed the possibilities and began seeking for something specific. But nothing came, nothing but that story of the lepers at the gates in 2 Kings.

Somehow, I found myself reading that story and understanding its perspective. I had no clarity about the future, but the past and present were like crystal. I was wasting away, making what seemed like negative progress toward my calling, my dreams, and divine design. Reflecting on my stagnation and cyclical behavior, I could perceive that there was real possibility that I'd continue walking in circles. I realized that if I didn't make some serious changes, the next five years could mirror the previous and maybe continue forever.

That fear of living, stuck for decades, finally overwhelmed the fear of moving out presumptuously. I went to my wife, and we began with one area. We had been stuck in multiple areas, but in this first one, we came together and headed towards where our hearts perceived life.

And God was gracious.

It wasn't even months or weeks that confirmation came. It was almost immediate. Life began to sprout. And growth continued and continued. :-)

Today, ugly and deceptive thoughts and emotions that create immobility and procrastination are still present. There is an ungodly language of suggestions and thoughts that is aggressive. It points out financial lack, scarcity, potential pitfalls, moral failures, and so on. I'm tempted to be self-reliant, perfect, or respond with anxiety. I'm tempted to promote my own discipline, spiritual authority, and financial mastery to silence the doubt and concerns.

But God is gracious.

I can now see through this trap.

I can see that everything that happens to me can either draw me closer to or further from God. Both success and failure are equally deceptive. And so overcoming lies and keeping my eyes on God has become the key to continually walking with God. I believe St. Augustine said it best with these words, "All things work together for good. Even sin." Or as the Apostle Paul puts it, "Nothing separates us from the love of God which is in Christ Jesus."

In every season, success or failure, there is provision made for us to remain connected, in the zone, and fruitful.

In every area of our lives, social, personal, professional, or ministry, God is there and we can enjoy him. Even when we have no idea what's happening, no clarity or even a scripture to rely on, He remains faithful.

I know many people have been hurt by negative experiences and have turned their backs on God. Life has not gone the way they hoped. And so, they have opted out from Christianity. And this greatly concerns me. My heart breaks for sons and daughters who've been hurt, lied to, and have turned away. The world we live in can provide a "god" or a belief system to fit every size, big or small. But I hope that you will remain faithful to the hope you first believed.

According to scripture, things are not getting easier. The deceptions are not decreasing. The lures and the options to gain fulfillment outside of Christ are multiplying. So I encourage you to remain and even grow tenacious to resist the lies that speak against the truth of Jesus Christ.

As Pastor Bill Johnson puts it, "I cannot afford to have a single thought in my head about me that God doesn't have in His."

God is bigger and better than we ever imagined Him to be.

My prayer for the few or the many who have read these words is that you will be equipped to continue walking with God, striving to know him better, and reflect him brighter.

If you have been stuck, I encourage you to deal with first things first. Reconnect your heart to your heavenly Father. Take a chance on love; test, taste, and see what's readily available. Realize the guilt and pain or even numbness is a lie trying to keep you distant.

If you need someone to pray with you or for you, please text me at +1 918–200–9572 or email mail@akcraig.com.

Blessings to you.

Create a Great Day!

Arvell Craig

## BONUS MATERIAL

My original plan was to have a 14-day devotional to go along with this book. I also wanted to create video resources to encourage dialogue and discussions on the material.

In order to avoid unnecessary procrastination, I decided to just publish what I had and worry about the other material later.

If you would like additional content related to this book, visit: www.SanctifiedAmbition.com/bonus.

# ABOUT THE AUTHOR

Arvell Craig has a Masters of Divinity, and has been an entrepreneur, associate pastor, church planter, adjunct professor, and now author. Currently, he produces the Monday Morning Devo Podcast, works for a technology company and is a workshop and keynote speaker to businesses and churches on personal and spiritual development.

Arvell resides in Tulsa, Oklahoma with his wife and daughter. For more information, please visit www.ArvellCraig.com.

# SANCTIFIED AMBITION

Made in the USA
Middletown, DE
27 April 2015